Music-Teaching Nursery Rhymes

By T.S. Cherry

Edited By Brenda Walker
IMPRINT: POP ACADEMY OF MUSIC

Music-Teaching Nursery Rhymes

A creative way to remember the keys on the piano

This book is a Music-Teaching Resource and can be used with our music-teaching system or combined with any other music-teaching system.

Pop Academy of Music

The Pop Academy of Music goal is to provide a wide range of tools and resources, including books and publications, to engage children of all ages in learning music theory concepts.

Sozo Music-Teaching System

Our easy-to-follow music-teaching system combines sight-reading and playing by ear. Techniques in retention of processes, concepts, and theories are taught using short stories, songs, animal characters, colors, and shapes that bring music to life for young musicians.

Musical Alphabet

Each white key has a name from the music alphabet.

Cat
Dog
Elephant
Fish
Giraffe
Ape
Bear

Pop Academy of Music

Read and Play Music

Sozo Music Teaching System

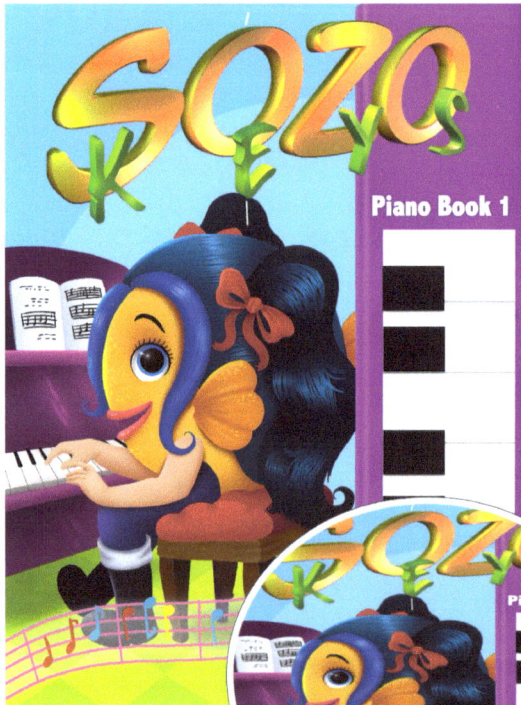

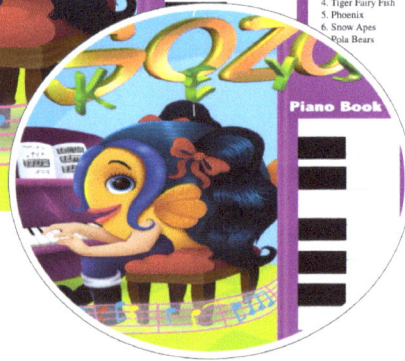

Black keys
1. Middleton Cats
2. Parkadians
3. Black Elephants
4. Merfish
5. Chromatic Apes
6. Graffiti
7. Dancing Bears

Red keys
1. Valentine-Revell
2. Kings
3. Pooka
4. Muddlefly Fish
5. Oracles
6. Flying Ares Apes
7. Sun Bears

Yellow keys
1. Chatty Cats
2. Map Dogs
3. Long Necks
4. Kissy Fish
5. Love me, Leave me
6. Green Giants
7. Berry, Berry Bears

Green keys
1. Emerald Cats
2. Winter Flower Dogs
3. Ele Emps
4. Tiger Fairy Fish
5. Phoenix
6. Snow Apes
7. Pola Bears

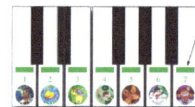

This box tells you the color of the piano keys.

4

Order your Piano Stickers Today

Black keys
1. Middleton Cats
2. Parkadians
3. Black Elephants
4. Merfish
5. Chromatic Apes
6. Graffiti
7. Dancing Bears

Red keys
1. Valentine-Revell
2. Kings
3. Pooka
4. Muddlefly Fish
5. Oracles
6. Flying Ares Apes
7. Sun Bears

Yellow keys
1. Chatty Cats
2. Map Dogs
3. Long Necks
4. Kissy Fish
5. Love me, Leave me
6. Green Giants
7. Berry, Berry Bears

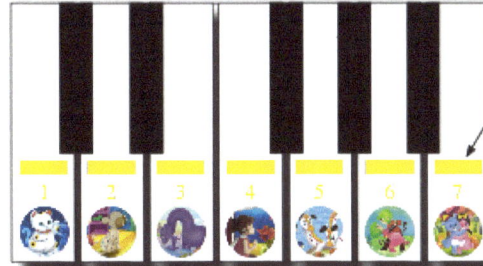

Green keys
1. Emerald Cats
2. Winter Flower Dogs
3. Ele Emps
4. Tiger Fairy Fish
5. Phoenix
6. Snow Apes
7. Pola Bears

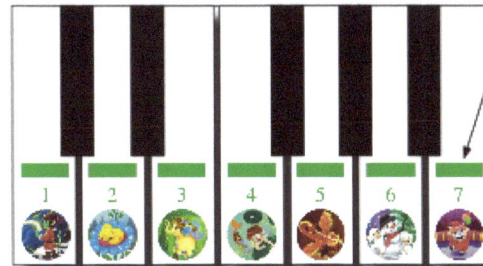

This box tells you the color of the piano keys.

Parkadian Dogs

Parkadian dogs
are from the human world, but they can talk
like you and me.
They founded a new world,
that teaches music
for all to see.

MERFISH

Right Hand Fish
Is the Merfish
4th black key
and they're teens

Fashion Divas
with legs and feet
and some of them
even have wings

Valentine - Revell Cats

A Valentine Male
Is a Le'Cat Tale
3rd space
of the Treble Clef

Use your right hand
first red key
His note is spelled
C-A-T

Chromatic Apes

The reflection I see
In front of me
Is not one that is myself
Are my eyes deceiving me
Or is this someone else?

I read a book
Then took a look
It's a magical tale to be found
I followed a trail of mirrors
to a cat wearing a crown.

Pooka

A Mischievous Creature
As old as time
A Pooka is red
And nine foot nine

Michael the Pooka

Michael played a trick
That caused him to be trapped
A witch cast a spell
never to be turned back

He used to be a boy
But never again
Now a mystical creature
Living in a foreign land

Oracles

Oracles have two heads
As you can see
Live on a distant planet
That has no rings
First moon from the sun
Offers the future and the past
Its called Exodus
The space above the staff

A Giraffe

A Giraffe can stretch his neck and sing
Only because of me
You reached and reached Graffiti City
But could never hit the G

Second line of the Treble Clef
Right hand 5th Black Key
I finally found my purpose
Hitting the note of G

Dancing Bear

The Dancers dance
To a song a four count magic square
Third line of the Treble Clef
Is the Dancing Bear

Seventh Black Key on the piano
Dancers dance fine art
Little dancers like Shirley temple
Are forever in your heart

KINGS

**Second Red Key
After the Cat
I am the King
As a matter of fact**

**Play me with your right hand
Then you'll see
That playing the King
Is playing the "D-O-G"**

Black Elephants

Trumpets are playing
The King has been crowned
Black Elephants are horns
Trumpet City
Is our town

First line of the Treble Clef
C-D
Then there's me
3rd Black Key on the piano
C-D
Then it's me

Muddlefly fish

Fish are always the 4th key
But my key is red
I fly in the bayou
Over everyone's head

I'm a Red Muddlefly Fish
A daydreamer of sorts
I pass the day by thinking
Of what's in the sea of quartz

www.ingramcontent.com/pod-product-compliance
Lightning Source LLC
Chambersburg PA
CBHW041557040426
42447CB00002B/202